It Came from Cambridge

Poems from people who live there.

Volume 2

FUSE

Fuse, https://www.fuseart.org/

ISBN: 978-1-998829-59-0

Acknowledgments

We would like to thank:

- Fuse, the arts group in Cambridge that supported the creation of this project;
- All the people who sent in their poems for consideration;
- The reviewers who gave their time and effort to read and comment on the poems that were submitted;
- Cambridge Authors Facebook Group for their support;
- Paul Langan for use of his images. All images in this publication, except page 21 and the Meet the Poet section, are from his collection.

About Fuse

Fuse is dedicated to making the arts more accessible in our local and global communities through the collaborative creation and presentation of Art. Their goals are to innovate the arts through modern technologies, educate our local communities through diverse programs, and actively identify and address stigmas in the arts. Fuse is a registered charity based in Cambridge, Ontario.
Visit fuseart.org for more information.

Table of Contents

Introduction

It is surprising that the city of Cambridge, with its rich history of the former towns of Galt, Hespeler and Preston, had never had a compilation book of short stories or poems by the authors who lived here.

A couple years ago, I joined the Cambridge Authors Facebook group and realized we had a dedicated group of local authors. It seemed logical that we would also have other authors in Cambridge that might not have published yet that were looking for a chance for their works to be published. In 2024, we published our first book – a collection of short stories from Cambridge authors. This book is volume 2 and features poems by local poets.

There is a registered charity arts organization in Cambridge called Fuse. Fuse had shown an interest in helping local writers.

Because I have a lot of experience in self-publishing, I volunteered to oversee both projects for Fuse.

I am proud of all the writers who submitted their poems.

Please enjoy reading these poems, and thanks for supporting our local Cambridge poets.

Paul Langan
Fuse Program Coordinator
March 7th, 2025

Snowstorm - Jaclyn Abrahams

The snow is falling
Like icy feathers it glides by
Pure white
Intricate designs
Not one is the same
They make everything look like new
Cleaning up everything in their path

Slowing life down in pace
A cold polar wind is blowing
Higher and higher
The banks grow
As small snowflakes fall
Staying where it's safe
Watching the storm clouds gather

I'm inside keeping warm
During the storm
Such wintry beauty
Fires up my mind
And inspires my imagination

Hot cocoa now gone
Listening to Nat King Cole's
"Stardust Melody"
I drift away
Once more
To the low moaning of the wind
Sweetest memories linger
In my dreams.

This Yearn of March - Becky Alexander

The rain blows in,
wind gusting,
puddles surging,
light buried deep in mist,
this heavy March morning.

I yearn for snowdrops,
crocuses, and hyacinths,
long for dew-drop shine
on blossoms and petals.

This moor-like dreariness
of 'too early' spring
prolongs winter, lets it
overstay its welcome,
leaves a grey and black pallor
in muddled curbside slush.

It is that sparkle
of renewed sunlight—missing,
that hopeful yearning of warmth,
and rebirth—
replaceable by nothing.

Westwind - John Anderson

Westwind was my forest playmate this morning.
She greeted my arrival
with gusty ruffling of my beard
and icy fingers that probed
under coat sleeves and pantlegs.
She teased my nostrils
with scents of pine and cedar
and blew snowflake kisses
across my cheeks.

Hide and seek was her game!
And though I never once saw her
I could tell where she hid
in the dancing trees
wakened from winter slumber
by her energetic romp through their branches.

A deep whisper through pines to my right,
then higher-toned sighs to the left
where leafless beech swayed to her rhythms
while dry-leaved oaks shivered a castanet percussion
And tall maples rubbed limb against limb
with moans and squeals
sighing the ecstasy of touch.

Then hushed silence,
an intake of air,
a stillness ...
Until her soft breath
and frosty kiss on my cheek
signalled that I, too,
had been invited to play.

Red Nose – Cynthia Ayres

A young child smiles at the Big Red Nose,
Watching eyes wide open as the balloon grows.
The child is so happy to be in this special place
With animals, popcorn and a clown's smiley face.

The bullied child wipes their Runny Red Nose,
As they run away from their fast, feisty foes.
Oh where can they go to find a small safe place,
So these bullies won't see those tears on their face.

The teenage child looks at their Bright Red Nose,
And wonders how they can get the smell of their clothes.
The child doesn't want others to know they are on drugs,
Or that they are involved with the neighborhood nasty thugs.

The child, no longer a child, looks with awe at the Red Nose,
And wonders, oh where, oh where, oh where the time goes.
It seems like only yesterday when looking at the clown's face,
The child saw the world as definitely a much happier place.

If only we could keep the innocence of the young child,
And the bullying and drugs were not so bold and wild.
Then this world would again be a happier, safer place,
And the child could keep that beautiful smile on their face.

A young child smiles at the Big Red Nose,
Watching eyes wide open as the balloon grows.

Soft Lace – Paul R. Bender

My love,
My life,
The song that beats
Beneath the skin of my chest
You are my dreams at night
My waking thoughts in sunlight
Those sublime melodies ringing through-out time
Your name, calling to me
Touching every inch
Of my quivering soul
As soft lace, whose stitches
Intertwine, remarkably

The City with Three Downtowns – Ken Doran

Beyond our city limits we boast we're from Cambridge with pride,
but in town we say it's Galt, Preston or Hespeler where we reside.
On lands purchased originally from The Six Nations, we give our thanks;
each locale developed and prospered on the Grand or Speed riverbanks.

Forced amalgamation in 1973 was to be a beneficial blending,
but for long-time residents it felt like a shotgun wedding.
Ominously, the next year the heavens opened causing the Grand to flood,
which left poor downtown Galt swamped with high water and mud.

Covering the largest portion, Galt blankets the southern half;
early settlers were Scottish, now Portuguese fill out the graph.
Industry flourished and saw stately homes built atop Dickson Hill;
there's also McDougall Cottage, Galt Collegiate, and Shades Mill.
Historic Galt Arena Gardens still hosts the annual School Skating Races,
so students can race laps where previous generations did their on-ice chases.

Preston and Blair cover the westside, settled by German-speaking Mennonites;
Settlers' Fork by the confluence of the Grand and Speed offers visual delights.

In the late 1800s the Preston Springs Hotel was renown worldwide;
now the towering silos of P&H Mills dominate the view by Riverside.
The Preston Rivulettes were led by Hilda Ranscombe, a superstar with the puck,
they dominated women's hockey of the 1930s with help from sisters Schmuck.
Built in 1837, the Lambs Inn in Blair was a stagecoach stop for Upper Canadians;
renamed Nicholson's Tavern, it had rolled ribs, pigtails and drunken shenanigans.
The hiking trails are beautiful around the hamlet of Blair,
a trio of which on the Charitable Reserve are considered quite *rare*.

The northeast side has Hespeler; founded by a businessman called Jacob,
whose mills and factories by the Speed provided the village its makeup.
Now known for its glass-enclosed library, Fashion Museum, and Mill Pond;
nearby at Four Fathers or Ernie's folks go for bevvies, bites and to bond.

Cambridge's scenery and cityscapes make for an ideal film backdrop,
so shows like The Handmaid's Tale and Murdoch Mysteries never flop.
Galt Hornets, Preston Jesters, Cambridge Hawks to Hespeler Shamrocks,
hockey here has a long and illustrious tradition that nobody knocks.
We have the Butterfly Conservatory, Hamilton Theatre, and Langdon Hall;

and now the exciting Gaslight District makes us feel like we have it all.
Besides an abundance of limestone buildings, pretty parks, and old mills,
Cambridge also has its share of steeples, bridges, and gently rolling hills.
For residents of The Bridge, there's no need to move elsewhere or to roam,
our motto says we're "a fine place for business, a great place to call home."
Not bad for the City with Three Downtown cores,
who amongst us could ask ... for anything more?

GALT COLLEGIATE INSTITUTE
HESPELER TOWN HALL
GALT TOWN HALL
SHEAVE TOWER BLAIR
WAR MEMORIAL PRESTON
CAMBRIDGE ONTARIO

No Thanks Mr. Donald - Jim Dyer

We thought you got the message
Two hundred years ago
We declined your offer then
and the answer still is no

We don't want to be
a fifty first state
in your mighty union
of prejudice and hate

So, No Thanks Mr. Donald,
Anyway thanks a lot
Sorry, we're not sorry
For not being who we're not

The Great State of Canada
was a notion in your head
more of your blah-blah-blah
that was better left unsaid

On one thing we agree
about this border so immense
we really now can see
that we do need a fence

So, No Thanks Mr. Donald,
Anyway thanks a lot
Sorry, we're not sorry
For not being who we're not

107

Crevices - Isabella Figueiredo

Nails will dig deep,
Into my bones, my darling.
In the moons deepest crevices I lay,
Although the lighting is dim during day.
I shall fall to my knees in such a weakness.
The snow mourns your name through sorrows, wing
Of broken stars fall gentle, and you will ring
So strong, the tears run from my saddened face
Blinking so slowly for I can see,
See a light through desolate airs, and
As petrified before you, your eyes stun me
Oh, how did I lose such a love throughout
The darkness of the endless night,
The moonlight may dance upon the lines in your face,
Forever beautiful, doused in grace.
I curse that it is not fair,
I pummel the dirt with my fury,
My fist filled with the scalp of the earth,
And beneath you I appear a child, weeping
For something that will now only visit in dreams.
How I wish we were two other people,
That I could hold you for longer,
And not lay in spaces,
I am far too big for now.
I am rocking away in the clefts of your absence,
Waiting for your call,
But until then, I will tell the moon,
How you were my greatest love of all.

Touched - Elaine Francis

Touched by love,
The inner beauty of our eyes,
The sacred warmth
Of a smile,
The haunting echo
Of our hearts.

Touched by pain,
Chaotic turmoil
Of the world
A constant yearning
Of our souls
Ever grasping for the light.

Touched by hope
Fragile hearts
Creep into the void
Through jagged cuts
All created
By a refusal to see

Touched by anger,
Throngs of people,
Baffled thoughts.
Meet the question of survival
When Hate clashes
With Love.

Touched by Love
Once again returning
Ever hopeful,
Ever yielding,
To heal the wounds
Of our sorrow.

The Job of a Dutiful Child – Sacha Geer

The job of a dutiful child is to be ever attuned to the swirling winds and changing weather of mood and tone.

She is never heard, and seen only in certain ways.

The dutiful child glows and is seen when she thrives in lack. When she flowers without water, without attention, without inquiry into her inner life.

Praise is never higher than when she is extraordinary flexibility, when she is charming deference, when she is quick witted and independent action for others.

The dutiful child neither has needs nor knows that needs are an option.

She does not challenge or tantrum, does not call in the middle of the night for want of water, or comfort from nightmares, or from a desire to be held and stroked.

A dutiful child is no bother - no nagging needed. An old soul. A wise beyond her years marvel.

A dutiful child is desperately lonely - and alone.

With pluck and support, a dutiful child grows to find her rage and her courage.

She finds her dusty needs and shows them tentatively first, then boldly. She holds the dutiful child tenderly, soothes her,

and heals.

The Cookie Tin - Jennifer Ann Gralec

pushed to the back
hidden behind
half-empty bottles and old chip bags
whose contents have long gone stale
beside the expired Avon books
selling promises of beauty
I see it
already tasting the sweetness on my tongue
I pull
move and rearrange
taking care to remember how everything was
only to find
after all that work
mis-matched buttons
and pearl tipped pins

Gratitude for Rust - Dan Ingrouville

If nothing stays perfect
did perfection ever exist at all
And what is perfection
but one person's ideal
The shabby age of materials
are my ideal
for they tell a tale of their existence
And like making it to yet another birthday
every patch of rust must be celebrated
Without the maintenance of one's idea of perfection
one may have time to think
Not think
Accept inspiration as it comes
and live as a piece of art and nature
As one that frays at the edge
because you have lived that long

The River - Jacki Langlois

I race along the path of The River on my new red three speed bike.
It was a gift – given in remorse, given in guilt, but given none the less.
It gives me freedom to outrun my thirteen-year-old self, my once clumsy gait replaced by soaring speed and glorious stride.

I catch my breath on the bench along The River, watching the water.
It flows and bubbles over sun drenched rocks creating little waves.
Ducks and geese glide and float and find their way kicking madly.
Little babies following in their mamas' strong and steady path.

The River watched me grow and stretch, reaching new heights.
As I grew from innocent child to reckless teen, to adult grown up me.
The River watched me run and play on endless summer days.
Underground mill works becoming our imaginary castles in faraway lands.

Those castles became our secret hiding spots – not always of this earth.
Long warm afternoons stretching into star lit nights, The River always alive.
Childlike wonder replaced by teen aged angst trying so hard to be what we never were.
Should I? Will he? What are they doing? It's time to go…

Later The River held my tears, my teen aged self, forced to grow too fast.
She is gone, she's no longer in pain, she's in heaven now.
But what about my pain, what about my heart – do not ask, just accept.
Smile and know in your heart that she is always with you…never enough.

Hand in hand, the bike long forgotten, he smiles at me – I'm nervous now.
Should I? Will he? Oh…it's not what I thought…kisses left wanting, caresses too awkward,
What is he doing? This doesn't feel right – it's time to go…
The River is aware, watching and telling me above all else, be true to myself.

That little baby boy, stroller bound but trying so hard to escape – The River calls him too.
The babbling of water over stones too much to ignore – he's out and running to greet it.
He runs little hands over rocks, the water rushing and cold, slick with beautiful coats of moss.
He smiles and our world bursts open. We turn and smile at each other both so in love with this gift.

Time ebbs and flows through the stories of our lives, like The River through the park.
Most days every day similar, some days beautiful, heart lifting, a few full of sorrow and pain.
Always triumphant, always rising after every fall. Always reaching out to pull each other up.
The River is there, always knowing, always sure, always showing the way home.

Buzz - Briana Lenzi

My lover; my Huckleberry;

He wears mustard shorts on a first date and walks a forested trail bathed in mosquitos, only for my company.

He nudges me aside so he may be closer to busy streets, his body of protection, my shield.

A shield, so wielding, it hovers close anytime my anxious mind wanders and frightens me into not trusting life.

How could I not have trust for a life that has led us to each other?

My head rests on his chest, the pulse of him reminds me miracles happen every day.

The ones filled with miraculous laughter.

The type that comes from jump scares and settling the score between them.

The type that comes with the over preparedness of "soapy napkins" at a picnic, one of us laugh crying in hysterics, the other revisits it anytime we pack a cooler.

The type that comes from play and a tickly moustache on a soft belly.

This love is alive, it buzzes like a wasps nest on a porch midsummer, tucked beneath shingles.

Neither of us are built to destroy such a masterpiece in progress.

We are both artists, this love, our medium.

Occasionally creating, occasionally cleaning up.

He says, "I fell in love with you on the trampoline", I blush, thinking of us bouncing and giggling. How our play is woven through these days like gold threads, adding spark and light to dull duties. How his laugh, his mischievous nature, reminds me of mine, and we feed off each other like those mosquitos on our first date.

I did not know healthy love until I experienced him.

His love, the rock I crash upon, the featherbed I fall into, the light that guides me back to myself, and the trust in love I have been missing.

He is, indeed, my Huckleberry.

The Quiet Skies - Taylor Lethbridge

The world's a stage; life, a bustling play,
Where each actor knows their lines by rote,
But mine's a script I can't quite seem to say,
A lilting cadence in each stress-wrought note.
So, I watch them weave their social tapestry
and yearn to join, but find no entry-key.

The tick-tock rhythm of their easy, verbal waltz,
An ebb-and-flowing current I don't dare to navigate,
My own thoughts echo, walled in by mental faults,
A silent language, sealed inside - my cruel and grueling fate.
The vibrant chaos of each day blinds and numbs my senses,
My words are set adrift and lost amongst its loud pretenses.

A symphony of noise and light, a blinding blaze, bedlam,
A spectacle of sound, and sight; a hammer to my brain,
A crash to hush each worthy thought before I've ever said them.
I miss the calm of solitude, awash in gentle rain.
The world's a canvas that's been drenched in jarring, noxious dyes,
While we happy few seek solace in the glow of quiet skies.

A mind, a maze of musings, mildly muddled, yet so bright,
Away from all the hubbub, is where brilliance bursts and blooms,
It's where senses swirl, and seek, and find, a special, sacred light,
Yet shadows stretch, and twist, and grow, in silent, empty rooms.

And kindness, even human touch, now feels like static's sting,
All my years of isolation show my mind's a fickle, fussy, thing.

Let in the world, the kaleidoscope of colours, bold and clashing,
Or stow away in solitude, a peculiar, private prison.
To choose between cacophony, and this lonely hell I've fashioned,
is to choose between my heart and mind, each day the sun has risen.
I long for something in between, with calm and human kindness
Somewhere to connect and feel, be mindful and not mindless.

One day, perhaps, I'll break on through my distant, stony guise,
Befriend the souls that walk alone beneath their quiet skies,
And free the beauty, hidden deep within my hazel eyes.

June 13th (Court Day – Me Too Edition) – Shannon MacKinnon

I've returned home from battle, Ma, I'm weak and worn.
I was tough, petrified, victorious and reborn.
In some eyes, I'm a hero! In others, I'm a witch!
Who blew the whistle of warning, a dirty, rat snitch.

Besmirched hands brewed, stirred, served and sold iniquitous lies.
Feeble souls listened, enlisted as enemy spies.
They slash in heavy fog, ignoring truth in my eyes.
My heart chose the mountain trail, where the sun loves to rise!

Mama, I am the resplendent Phoenix sizzling bright.
I transformed into my own hero, my own knight!
And I chose to be courageous, to shine in the dark.
To showcase character, leave an indelible mark.

My dear sisters have been noosed at work for far too long.
I mounted onto my dark horse and held my sword strong.
I charged into battle unaware of my blind fate.
With a calm composure, ignored the enemy's bait.

After a tiring combat, my adversaries fled.
Cheering and hollering, the ground streaked in crimson red.
Ma, I won a war I never enlisted to fight.
I'm a damsel reborn into a warrior knight.
And in the face of evil, I chose to be the light!

Thomas and Milo - Dan McQuain

Thomas and Milo did not understand
the blessings that abound;
the kindness,
the comfort
and warm loving hugs.
The peace of their childhood town.

Thomas and Milo did not understand
The morals that made right
the hellwinds,
the carnage
as shrieking bombs fell.
The screams of their neighbors that night.

Thomas and Milo did not understand
their mother was so chill,
her stiff hands,
her silence,
her glazed empty stare.
Her warm heart forever now still.

Thomas and Milo did not understand
the strangers dressed in brown;
who shouted,
who trampled,
who searched everywhere.
And killed everyone that they found.

Thomas and Milo had quite quickly learned
search corpses of the dead
take water,
take canned goods
and ignore the smell
And to hide in the homes they had fled

Thomas and Milo had quite quickly learned
The lessons taught by war:
move softly;
talk lowly;
no friendship or faith
And a hatred that burns to the core.

Thomas and Milo did not understand.

A Request - Neelofar Naheed

I have a request, my kids,
Before it's too late and I become too weak to speak.

Can I have a clear blue sky, without any patches of pollution?
It's covering the sun, holding back the sunlight, affecting my vision.
The rain is so acidic, my soil has lost its pH levels.

I don't smell the sweetness of mud anymore when it rains and water dwells,
My guards, the trees and mountains have been slaughtered,
There are very few of them left to hold my underground water,
The rivers and lakes are drying now, what is left, has become a dumping ground.

Can I have clean water without the heaps of plastic and tyres and nuclear waste?
I know you have water filters, but my biological processors are dying,
The water is so poisonous to taste.

Technology is booming, and you are on top of the food chain,
The population has exploded, and I am unable to retain,
I am too old to adapt and need a little attention for sure,
Because it is rightly said that prevention is better than cure.

I know that you are looking for other planets to plant your life,
You are all my kids, and I want you to survive,

So, I request you, till you find a new home, please keep me alive.

Evolution, adaptation, species, the cycle of life, death and birth
For millions of years, holding it all together

I am MOTHER EARTH.

Life from the loam – Nathan Pirie

It has been watching
through primordial eyes
from jeweled crowns to Six Nations
never wondering why
until coins marked its face
as listed, purchased, and sold;
they built houses and churches,
looking up, growing old.

For life from the loam
sees things quite differently
it knows of heartbeats in earthen chests
of roots reaching evermore,
of all things that came before,
for it hears heartbeats that have never left.

Decay is slow and memories are rebirth,
a reminder that all life is born of the earth,
destined to return, yet we build higher each year
with a childish sneer, "you can't catch me up here."

A flaw of perception perhaps
or an unruly need to outpace
natural order and mindful growth—
yet to truly learn our place.

Still, it has been watching
ever with Renewed Hope
but it too has been learning
perceiving spectrum and scope:
how to build, what is love,
lessons of heart and of home—
lessons only learned.... when built up from the loam.

Jesse James - Brier Pomfret

Ghosts of steam dissipate into the afterlife through skeletal branches above;
Cries of metal scraping against metal emit from a mouth of sparks, igniting the darkness.
Blood pumps through a roaring heart of coal and fire,
Giving life to electric lights that cast shadows of tree trunks, dim and long,
Turning them into temporary sundials as they pass.
Time is in motion.
Speeding up
Then slowing down.

I stand unseen, a figure in the wings, waiting for my cue,
Unmoved by the bellowing charge of the locomotive, wrought of cold iron.
A deafening silence, the infinite stillness of waiting, ringing in my ears,
Choking my soul from my body, eating me alive
Until all that remains is but a shattered reflection staring back with a predator's eyes.
A hunter lying in wait.
A monster that should not be, yet is.
A nightmare turned real.

Enveloped in the deep shadow, I become a background:
Imperceivable,
Patient.
Hungry.

A sigh of sorrow echoes through the woods as the train heaves to a stop,
Shrouded by the last breath of a dying fire.
Anticipation clings to the air, pressing against me in a thick, humid fog,
I step into the light.

It’s time to move.
Time to take.
Time to kill.

A Prison of Flesh – Navjot Ranu

I wake up to the numbness of a body that's no longer mine,
And this silence so thick that it drowns out time.

I talk to my hands, my legs, and my skin,
But there's no answer, no echo, and no movement within.

The ceiling stares down at me, unbothered by my plea,
While gravity mocks what I once thought was free.

Breathe…just breathe, I tell myself as I try to take control,
While I'm fighting the chaos that's seeping through my soul.

Terror, such terror, it grows in my chest,
It's a vine of despair that won't let me rest.

Time drips slowly, merciless and unkind,
Every second a dagger digging into my fractured mind.

I'm stuck, hopeless and helpless, caught in its snare,
Frozen in fear while I'm gasping for air.

This panic, it rises, clawing in my throat,
It's a feral scream that just can't find its note.

I'm locked in this cage, this body, this bed,
It's a coffin for the living, and I'm a soul left for dead.

No hope, no light, no path to take,
Just the betrayal of a body I can no longer wake.

What if this is forever, this prison of flesh,

These questions are suffocating, they're cruel and
they're fresh.

As I lie in sinking, shifting sands,
I realize my life is no longer in my hands.

In that moment, the truth is clear,
I am my prison, and I am my fear.

Empty Shells – Monica Sedra

Illusions of beauty. Smooth curves, light tones. Picked up, thrown away.
It's just an empty shell.

Listen closely, what do you hear? Are there waves? Is it silence?
Once lived in, but no longer. Only a faded memory now.
It's just an empty shell.

Deep blues, strokes of green. The abrasive sand takes over.
Place your shell where you like. Shelf it, bury it, break it even, don't think twice.
A funeral, all the same.
It's just an empty shell.

Once moving, once colourful. Now vacant, somber, and still.
All that's left is a remembrance of what was, what may never be again.
What changed? Who changed?
Perhaps it was always an empty shell.

Look closely, you'll see. Who lived inside has left for good, whether for an upgrade or a goodbye.
Does it wait for a new host? Is it waiting for the old? Will it hold life once more?
I hope it's possible, I pray it's possible.

But yet again, plans might never come to be.
After all, it's just an empty shell.

Looking At Life Through the Eyes of a Child - Bianca Siciliano

I still love to colour.
I still love to paint.
I love playing games.
I think it's just great.

Popcorn and movies
Are such a great time.
I'm still sometimes messy.
I think it's just fine.

Lounging in my pajamas
Is something I like to do.
I still stay up late
Watching a rerun or two.

I'm just saying that
I am no longer a child.
But it's important to have fun.
Sometimes, for a little while.

There is magic in the sunrise.
The vast glow of the moonlight.
And will remember when things get tough as we grow,
That there is always kindness in others.
A helping hand to hold.
Our inner child still sees the Beauty of the World.

It's Not Goodbye – Jennifer Stoliker

See you later, see you soon
See you next time, see you then and
See you around, all mean the same thing,
But it's not goodbye.

Take care, keep in touch
Speak to you then, talk to you later and
Until then, all mean the same thing,
But it's not goodbye.

Adios, ciao
Arrivederci, farewell and
Cheers, all mean the same thing,
But it's not goodbye.

Ta-ta, so long
Sayonara, cheerio and
Later, all mean the same thing,
But it's not goodbye.

Toodle-oo, toodle pip,
Pip pip, laters and
Ta-ra, all mean the same thing,
But it's not goodbye.
And even as I bid you adieu…it's not goodbye.

If Nobody Smiled – George W. Tebbs

If nobody smiled a smile at me,
And only the sombre face I see,
I'd drift away from the haunts of men,
To seek the joys of the fairy glen,
And in the basket that nature weaves,
I'd gather up smiles from flowers and leaves.

If nobody shared their light with me,
I'd dance with moonbeams wild and free,
And catch the twinkle of starlit skies,
To plant them deep where sadness lies,
For in the darkest hour of night,
Nature's smile burns ever bright.

If nobody's warmth could reach my heart,
I'd let the gentle breeze impart,
Its whispered secrets sweet and low,
Of places where wild roses grow,
And there among the nodding trees,
Find friendship in the summer's breeze.

If nobody's joy could touch my soul,
I'd watch the ocean's rhythmic roll,
And learn from waves that laugh and play,
How happiness finds its own way,
For nature's children understand
Those smiles are gifts upon this land.

The Wonder of Everything - Ruth Thompson

Do trees wonder as I wonder?
Why is there wind and rain and fire?
Why are there seasons?
Why do we crumble and fall?

And the deeper questions
Why am I here?
What is my purpose?
What lights my path?

Do trees reveal the mystery?
Swaying splendor, sighing contentment
Perfection of leaf and branch
Connected to earth and air and water

The urgency of spring sprouting
The autumn colours' fall
The frigid slumber endured
The wonder of rebirth

All say there is a rhythm and a reason
For everything

The One - Addison Tkaczyk

Found the woman of my dreams
On the internet
Sunday night, she had my heart
Though we never met
I ask her out, Friday night,
The date is set

Oh, how it goes
Guess she'll never know

She chose to get away, her loss
They say happens to us all
Still hurts 'till this day

Couple months, finally pass
Ready to search again
I pray to find, my future wife
I swipe, I swipe, again

Meet a lady, really sweet
She's pretty keen on me
We laugh and joke, but she is
not the one for me

I wish her well, I tell her that
Respectfully
She understands and appreciates
My honesty

I do not ghost, I do not hide
My Mum raised a good son

I wish you all well
I pray we all
Find the one

Rerouted - Amanda Tkaczyk

This is what is
No joyfulness or hurt
It's the end of this road
Paths must diverge

You're going east, I'm facing west
In each other's rear-view mirror
While we wish each other best

We'll keep rolling along
Winding thru the night alone
And on our way towards anew

This pit stop is closing shop
We've gathered what we want
And carefully discarded
All the rest

You head east, I head west
I will be thinking of this detour
And my broken GPS
Wondering when you finally
Make it to the sea
If anything you see
Will make you think of me

A stranger whose path
We shared along the way
Until the end of this road
The end of this road

The comment section is lonely, when everyone's an influencer – Steffan Williams

Celestial bodies spin predictable,
Ellipses. They spin solitary
With others
You're a rapt voyeur

From faded threadbare cushions
you slowly raise a glass to your lips
Three fingers of something
Using its legs to slide down
The sides of the glass

You watch lying constellations
pretending to creep
Across the night sky
In reality they leave
moon dust in their wake
they rush to splash
In the milky way

Dairy displacement is nonexistent
Cinematographers can't be
Swimming partners
Or friends
They're busy
planning the next scene

Meet our Poets

A-Do

Jaclyn Abrahams - I started to write poetry over 35 years ago as a teenager. My grade 10 teacher, Ms. Dian Bell encouraged me to continue writing which I did progressively. It took the pandemic to create an opportunity to gather together those writings into a book entitled, "Scattered Leaves" which is available on Amazon.ca.

Becky Alexander - is a writer and poet. She has written two memoirs about growing up in Hespeler. Her poetry has been published in seven countries and has won hundreds of awards. She operates Craigleigh Press, a micro-publishing company that has published the works of over twenty deserving writers.

John Anderson – is a retired Psychotherapist & Pastor, certified Forest Therapy guide, 4 adult children, 10 grandchildren & 2 great-grandchildren. Recently remarried (to Evelyn.) Likes to spend his time hiking, geocaching, communing with friends (both human & more-than-human,) & occasionally writing down his thoughts & feelings about the world around us which gives us shape & flavour.

Cynthia Ayres - I have lived in Cambridge most of my life. One of my passions is Toastmasters as it has allowed me to present speeches, mentor others and learn and grow my communication and leadership skills outside of school. I have written many poems and one book but up until now have not pursued having them published even though it has been on my bucket list for a long time. Being chosen to be part of this publication is an honor for me that I feel will motivate and encourage me to share more of my other pieces of work.

Paul R. Bender – - was born and raised in Kitchener, Ontario, Canada among the rolling hills, south of the old order Mennonite farms of Waterloo Region. He currently resides in Hespeler, now part of Cambridge Ontario with his wife of twenty years and son.
Paul spends most of his time paddling his canoe along the eddies or bends on the Speed River at the face of his home or hours pecking letters to words while dreaming of wilderness trips with his wife.

Ken Doran - *The City with Three Downtowns* is Ken's first poem to be published. His book *My Canadian Hockey Journey* was published in 2021 and his second one *Pleasantly PSYCHOTIC* will be released this year. The married father of two lives in Cambridge.

Dy-I

Jim Dyer - made Cambridge his permanent home in 2003. With him came his passion for folk music, both for listening and to play. By 2010 his attention increasing shifted towards his own lyrics. Since then, he has learned that not all lyrics are meant to be songs, and many are better left as poetic reflections and commentaries.

Isabella Figueiredo - I grew up here in Cambridge and have been writing poetry for about 4 years. I'm sixteen, and I have always found solace in speaking my feelings through writing. It is a beyond-physical comfort space, and something I adore greatly.

Elaine Francis - Her interests include music, psychology, counselling, and human rights.
She enjoys writing short stories, poetry and has completed a novel. Elaine hails from Toronto, but now calls Cambridge, Ontario her home.

Sacha Geer - When she was about 6, Sacha's aunt gave her a card that said, 'you are a lover of words, one day you'll write a book'. Nearly 40 years later she is still working at that, scratching away at poems and prose in her spare time at her home in Preston. She's happily lived there since 2008 with her two cats and delightful partner, Drew. The cats strongly prefer Drew to her - can't win 'em all.

Jennifer Ann Gralec - lives in Cambridge (Hespeler) Ontario, with her husband Arthur and their two children, Aster and Emma. Earning her Honours English Degree in 2000 from Wilfrid Laurier University (Waterloo), Jennifer spent the first decade after graduation in sales until deciding to walk away from a successful career to open a little bakery in Downtown Galt.
When not busy baking cupcakes and sweet treats, she writes poetry and prose exploring themes of love, loss, beauty and the human condition.

Dan Ingrouville - is a visual display artist, local choreographer, photographer and since 2018, an avid poet. Many of his poems are inspired by his photographs.
Originally from Toronto, Dan and his wife, Jane, moved to Cambridge in 1988 to raise their two daughters, Kaelyn and Madeline. Much of Dan's inspiration has come from Cambridge and its community of clever citizens.

L-N

Jacki Langlois - I am a born and bred Cambridge resident with family roots in Newfoundland. I've always admired my father's ability as a storyteller and often hoped people saw me in a similar light. For me, writing is a back and forth kind of dance that dabbles in stories, poetry and prose as I try to honour those I love and my own heart...

Briana Lenzi - is an artist and poetry writer known for creative works that express the expansiveness of human experiences. She has a passion for exploring the vastness of polarity and how it emerges in daily life. Her latest book, *Discombobulated Constellations*, draws on extensive personal experience of an authentic journey. She encourages creativity to all humans, in whatever form is most therapeutic and meaningful to them.

Taylor Lethbridge – is a luthier, lover, lyricist, painter, poet, photographer, and Santa's favourite helper—a true multi-hyphenate. Autistic and authentically himself, he pours his unique perspective into every creation, transforming wood, canvas, words, and light into works of art. When he's not busy puttering, you can find him watching Scooby Doo with his dog, Bailey.

Shannon MacKinnon - is an actress and creative who has been fortunate to appear in shows like "How To Die Alone" (Disney Plus) and "Cursed Histories" (Super Channel). She has also been a host for Toronto International Autoshow, RunwayTO Toronto and Cable 14 Hamilton Limited. She is very grateful to be a part of this volume. Follow her on
Instagram @Shannondmackinnon

Dan McQuain - was a dog trainer for 40 years. He trained drug dogs, bomb dogs and guard dogs. He left the position as the operations manager of a security company to follow his twin lifelong dreams of being a car salesman and a writer. Now semi-retired, thanks to covid, he is a first aid instructor and still plugging away at being a writer.

Neelofar Naheed - I have been living in Cambridge for the past 5 years and have fallen in love with the charm of Galt. An Engineer by Profession and a Yoga/fitness instructor by passion.

P-S

Nathan Pirie - is an author, translator, and bookbinder. His formal education is in French literary studies from the University of Waterloo, and his creative work is influenced by his passion for language, fantasy, and the natural world. A blend of environmentalism and fantasy realism, he published *Leviathan* in 2022 (Highwind Press), which is the first collection in the *Personal Mythologies* series—an exploration of self and heritage through the lens of world mythologies and the innate magic of nature.

Brier Pomfret - is a husband, Dad, and Behaviour Analyst who loves to play music, hike, and write the occasional poem in his spare time.

Navjot Ranu - Writing for me was a hobby that turned into a passion. While living with a disability, it's helped me put motionless emotions that I and countless people may have felt, into words.

Monica Sedra - Hi, I'm Monica. I like my coffee black, my music loud, and God working in the centre of my life

Bianca Siciliano - Originally from the GTA, my husband Peter, my cat Dinah and I moved to Cambridge to get away from the hustle and bustle of the city – we have never looked back. I work remotely for a Non-Profit Organization focusing on food security & Education Programs in countries such as Uganda, Ghana & Indigenous Communities in Canada. I enjoy making others feel welcome and listening to other people's stories. I credit my Italian Heritage and the upbringing of my parents (especially my mother) for instilling my desire in helping others realize their full potential and for my love of literature, writing & the arts.

Jennifer Stoliker - I am 49 years old and have lived in Cambridge all my life. I work fulltime in a local hotel where I manage the housekeeping department there. I like to be in or on the water, so in the summer you can find me at one of many surrounding beaches. I love photography and take pictures of everything, but what I love most is to write. I have been writing poetry since I was 13 years old. It is my outlet. Sometimes I find it easier to express myself on paper. Writing comes easily and naturally, and I hope one day to publish a book. This is just the beginning.

T - W

George W. Tebbs – was the first superintendent of the Coombe home in Hespeler, ON from 1905-1913. Smyly Homes in Ireland sent children to the Coombe for a better life. George went on to become a popular minister due to his radio show on CKOC. He did over 3000 radio broadcasts of his Old Man Sunshine show. Lifting the spirits of many, especially during the depression years. This poem comes from a rare booklet of poems from the 1930s.

Ruth Thompson - is a Holistic Nutritionist with twenty-one years in private practice in Cambridge. She has two self-published books about holistic health
and a short story in It Came from Cambridge. Volume 1. The Wonder of Everything was inspired by her long-

time fascination with the big questions of life that often go unanswered. This is her first published poem.

Addison Tkaczyk - is a music artist, songwriter, and producer who creates catchy and emotional songs. He makes music that tells stories and connects with people. His songs mix R&B, pop, and hip-hop to bring a fresh and exciting sound. You can listen to his music on YouTube and Spotify at Mr. Soundtrackz.

Amanda Tkaczyk - is an emerging multi-media artist based in Galt. Previous slam poetry competitor at the Canadian Festival of Spoken Word and award-winning digital artist and photographer at the Cambridge Fall Fair, Amanda brings together her accessible rhythmic poetry, chaotic abstract paintings, and bizarre digital art to create compelling emotional experiences. You can find her art on Instagram @whatsoever_creates

Steffan Williams - is a Caribbean-Canadian poet based in Cambridge, Ontario. He draws inspiration from the harmonics of music and the rhythms of nature, weaving verses that illuminate the beauty of life's quiet moments.

It Came from Cambridge Vol. 1 – Short stories from people who live there

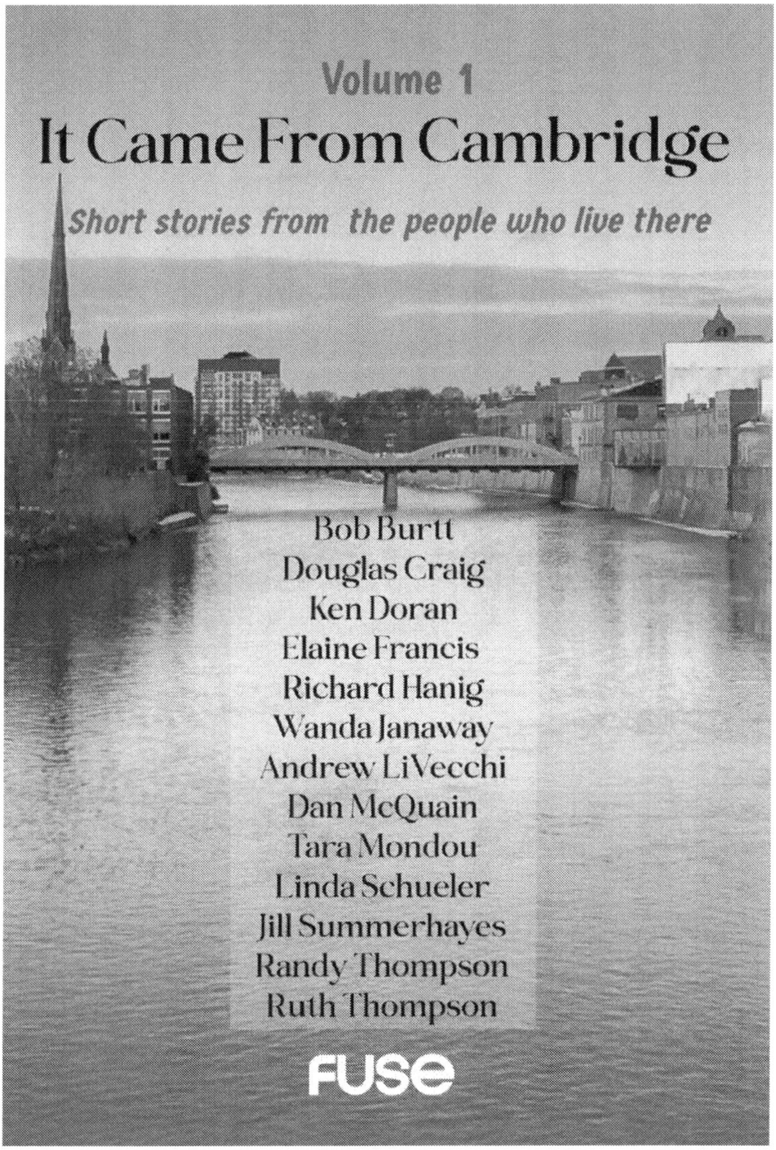

(Released in 2024)